The T̶ ̶ ̶ ̶ ̶
Breaking Free From A Negative Thought Life

Second Edition

To Karen,
Thanks for
supporting me!

Sharon Blake

Life Chronicles Publishing
Give your life a voice!

http://www.lifechroniclespublishing.com
Life Chronicles Publishing
ISBN-13: 9780692641910
Cover Design:
Life Chronicles
Editor:
Maleeka T Holloway and Debrena Jackson-Gandy
Life Chronicles Publishing Copyright © 2018

Dedication

To My Creator - for guiding me to see the truth.
My children, Vashon, Jasmin, and Darius, whom I love dearly.
Thank you for your patience as I find my truth.

A special thank you to Dr. Caroline Leaf for inspiring me to
examine my thought life.

Contents

Foreword

The Thought Detox book by Sharon Blake provides the reader with first-hand insight into the truth of toxic thinking.

Sharon reveals practical insights and gives you a deeper understanding of the "Why and How" toxic thoughts impact a person's life journey. The drama and trauma of toxic relationships can lead to a multitude of emotional, physical, relational, and spiritual maladies.

This book not only identifies the underlying roots of "Toxic Thinking," but also lays out a pathway to move from being a victim to becoming victorious. Sharon unpacks the specific consequences of toxic thoughts, which have the potential to immobilize a person from fulfilling their destiny in life.

She knows what it feels like to experience negative, critical, and sabotaging thinking. These negative thoughts go underground yet, create havoc "above ground" in a person's life and relationships.

Sharon keeps it real when exposing the reality of decisions that kept her stuck for many years. She shares with the reader the perseverance, accountability, and ownership necessary to navigate the journey to freedom. This book challenges you to pursue your identity and refute lies such as, "You will never amount to anything."

She compassionately and honestly speaks to the intentional choices needed to break free of generational cycles, patterns, and negative thinking.

Answering the reflection questions and utilizing journal writing will assist you in applying key principles in your life. Be encouraged that you will become more than a conqueror.

I pray Sharon's book will take you on the journey to healing and deliverance. May her grace-filled words set you free from a negative thought life and permit you to "Detox."

-Dariel Brown
Licensed Therapist, Certified Life Coach, Addiction Specialist, Human Behavioral Consultant

Introduction

We will be working on identifying negative emotions and thoughts; they can be any negative, worrisome, irritating, and or shameful thoughts or feelings. Toxic and negative thoughts are thoughts that must be dug up and replaced with healthy new thoughts. You can learn how to identify these thoughts and retrain your mind to think anew. However, to find out what we really believe we must sift through our thoughts. I thought that I knew what I believed. However, I found through careful examination of my thought life, there were some very toxic beliefs I had concerning myself and others. Ones I never knew existed! This process will not happen overnight, but change will occur over time.

Please seek professional help if you feel you need it.

As you begin you may feel uncomfortable, a natural part of the process where some individuals may want to give up. If change is what you seek then feeling uncomfortable will be a natural occurrence of this process. Remember to take care of yourself on this journey. Give extra attention to how you feel and allow yourself grace and time to take a break if you need it. This is a journey, not a race.

Write down the negative thoughts that you struggle with. Negative thoughts usually start with *I can't, I am no good, I will never, I won't make it through this, and I am afraid to do.* They include internal critical thoughts of yourself or others. These types of mental messaging and beliefs keep you from becoming aware of the need for change. If you choose not to be a part of the healing process, you will succumb to these thoughts and beliefs. Allow yourself to recognize the untruths and negativity to become more aware of what is actually going on in your thought life.

Here are some questions to ask yourself while going through this book. So, grab a journal and let's get started.

- Where do these thoughts originate?

- Who comes to mind when these thoughts are present?

- What emotions are associated with these thoughts?

- How do you feel about yourself when these thoughts are present? Guilt? Shame? Anger? Anxiety? If feelings of guilt and shame arise don't stop. There is more work to be done. We must learn to move past the feelings of guilt and shame for healing to occur.

- What purpose do these thoughts serve? If our thoughts are not serving a good purpose, we must get rid of them and rectify the reasons for their existence.

You may need help with this from a counselor, pastor, or friend. It is ok to ask for help. This book will not diagnose you.

Begin to re-train how you think by replacing old negative thoughts with new healthy thoughts. Once you have identified the toxic thoughts and emotions, then it is time to examine and expose those thoughts for what they really are. The process of analyzing what is going on in your mind is very necessary for change to occur. For example, if your negative thought is, "No one loves me" or "It's too hard to change," you will immediately say, "I LOVE myself enough to change," when these thoughts try to rear their ugly head.

We will allow ourselves to feel what we feel concerning those thoughts but do not stay focused on the negative. It is imperative that we exchange old toxic thoughts with new life-giving thoughts that will aid in creating a new life. When the negative thoughts come up again, "control-alt-delete" them.

Control - I will Control thoughts that I allow into my mind. (Breath In)

Alt - I will Stop the negative impact of the toxic thoughts. (Exhale)

Delete - I will Replace all negative/toxic thoughts by replacing them with positive, life-giving thoughts (Breath In)

Now, it is not enough to just recite affirmations about your thoughts and your circumstances; you must take ownership of new healthy ideas. Taking ownership is taking possession of your new thoughts through affirming, visualizing, and feeling.

As you write, pay close attention to what you are feeling. Recognize how you feel and write about other experiences that have made you feel the same way. This is important to get down to the root of your negative thought process that continues to occur. You may find that some of what you feel originates from past junk that has nothing to do with your current situation. However, the mere reminder of the past hurt can trigger those emotions to surface in your current situation. Do your emotions warrant what you are experiencing today?

Uncovering the truth is necessary for healing to occur. Replace the lies with the truth you find. Use scriptures and affirmations to counter what your negative thoughts are telling you to think and feel.

Here are a few affirmations and scriptures for you to recite daily.

I AM ENOUGH

I AM LOVED

I AM COURAGEOUS

I AM WORTH IT

I AM SUPPORTED

I AM NOT ALONE

I CAN DO THIS

I AM POWERFUL

I CAN BE ACCOUNTABLE TO MYSELF WITHOUT OWNING GUILT AND SHAME

I AM A TRUTH SEEKER

I WILL OWN THE TRUTH NO MATTER HOW HARD IT MAY BE

I AM FEARFULLY AND WONDERFULLY *MADE Psalms 139:14(NIV)*

Chapter One
Taking Ownership IN the Truth of You

I decided to write this book based on my own personal experience. In my first book, *Chronicles of Pain,* I gave my readers an inside view of my life to show how important it is to release the pain of the past in order to move forward in life. In the past, I was always on "auto-pilot." I did what I was taught or raised to do without really questioning. I never put much brainpower into pondering the "whys" of my actions and decisions. I just did what I was told to do by family and those closest to me.

One day, after carefully examining where I was in life, I concluded something was wrong with the way I perceived myself, others, and my environment. I had a distinctly negative mindset. My negative mindset led me to make the wrong choices about the people I allowed into my life and the places I decided to visit. Everyone I knew, including myself, seemed angry, fearful, and confused for reasons no one seemed to talk about. We had no clear direction. We simply existed. As I began to look at myself and the company I kept, the more dysfunction I saw. I knew I would need divine intervention and guidance to make some critical and necessary changes. I became weary of settling for "good enough" when in my heart of hearts, I knew I deserved "the best."

I began to pray and ask God to show me what I needed to do to change my life, those prayers led me to research how behavioral habits are formed. After searching for answers, God revealed to me that it was my mindset that needed to change. Because of how my life had unfolded, I needed to search for the truth outside of what I was taught to believe. I soon learned everything I had been through - the good, the bad and the ugly - had a purpose. But what was my purpose? When I allowed myself to believe there could be more to my life than what I knew, the doors of opportunity opened for me.

Since then, I have learned a great deal about myself and why I once navigated my life the way I did. Living my life without true purpose kept me making the same tragic decisions and ending up in repeated horrible situations. I was in the same broken, dysfunctional relationships and I was tired of "merry go round" results. I finally screamed to my inner conscience, "Let me off!"

I was over spinning my wheels without getting to a destination. It was time for me to deal with me. I asked myself two important questions, "Who am I?" and "Who gave me the idea I had to be what I had become?" I was always searching for something or someone to fulfill me. I began to realize, and accept, who I had become was a direct result of my healthy and unhealthy beliefs. Once I started to uncover those hidden thoughts, beliefs, and thinking habits, I discovered where I needed to focus my attention for healing. Some of those toxic beliefs were: *I will never be good enough, I must settle for less, I will always have to do the hard work because of the color of my skin.* This process allowed me to see and accept both the ugly and beautiful sides of me. As I began piecing together the puzzle of my emotional life, I realized how much work I needed to do. I took ownership of my negative thinking, allowed myself to feel uncomfortable with the guilt of my mistakes, applied forgiveness to all who had hurt me—including myself.

Throughout this book, you will identify toxic emotions and thoughts that limit you from reaching your fullest potential. Unhealthy thoughts are what I consider to be illegitimate thoughts. They should not be permitted to exist in our minds. These are thoughts that have possibly formed without our understanding of the damage they yield. These negative ways of thinking must be recognized, removed, and replaced with new more positive thoughts. I like to say we are going to learn how to control-alt-delete these thoughts.

I have included questions at the end of the chapters. Take time to write your answers. As you are writing, pay close attention to what you are feeling. After you have recognized how you feel write about other experiences that have made you feel the same way and ask yourself the hard question, *why do you feel the way you do?* Is what you feel today relevant for today or are your feelings rooted in past hurt? To acknowledge what you are feeling is the beginning of the process of breaking free from a negative thought life. It is important to get to the root of the negative emotion. In doing this, we will find the negative thought that is driving the negative emotion.

This process will not happen overnight, but change can and will occur if you are willing to dig deep and put forth the work required to change your thought life. Change will push you to open your mind to new possibilities and belief systems. *Remember that beliefs are the roots of thoughts. BELIEFS are deeply rooted and anchored in our minds, and we treat them as "truth" whether they are true or not.*

Some of these thoughts you may have chosen to forget or have chosen to believe that they have not adversely affected you. However, the process of change requires truth and honesty. We will need to be ready to accept the truth concerning our thoughts and beliefs. Are your beliefs the truth or not?

Getting honest with yourself first, then with others, is a necessary part of the detoxing from negativity and toxicity process. For me to overcome my faulty belief systems, I needed to accept that many of my beliefs were not true and much of what I was feeling today had nothing to do with my current experiences. I needed to be honest about who I am today and take ownership of *why* I am who I am today. This takes truth and honesty. If you do not like truth, you will have a hard time breaking free from your negativity. There are many reasons why we won't take ownership of our *junk*. It is not easy at first. We will address some of these reasons in future chapters.

This book is a story of the process and the tools I have used to recognize false thoughts and beliefs in order to become the *conductor* of my thought life. It was the beginning of taking my life back. I hope this book encourages you on your journey of detoxing from a negative thought life.

Often, we do not know where to start the *digging* process. Use these questions as a guide to uncover your truth.

Questioning Myself...

Who do I think I am?

Can I accept truths outside of what I have grown up to believe?

Am I open to questioning and challenging my belief systems?

Who told me who I needed to become? Who do I believe I
am?

Do you like you? Why? or Why not?

Who instilled this belief system embedded into my heart and soul?

Have my past negative life experiences dictated my behavior
for far too long?

When I was I child, my thoughts/beliefs were being created. Are
those thoughts/beliefs even true today? Have these thoughts
created a toxic belief system?

A production of thoughts in my mind and heart came to life and
caused me to be. Who am I a product of?

Am I a by-product of lies and untruths?
Does my privilege blind the true reality of myself and others?

Am I biased? What do those biases allow me to do or not do?

Am I even aware of my biases?

Was I conceived in dysfunction and turmoil?

Am I surrounded by dysfunction? How has that dysfunction shown up in my life?

Have I become the child of despair, fear, and anxiety?

Do I see the truth of who I have become? Am I ignoring the truth of who I have become?

WHAT IS the truth of who I have become?

Chapter Two
Identity Crisis

Now that we have started to uncover why we are the way we are, lets dive into who we truly are.

Identity is defined as the conceptions, characteristics, beliefs, and expressions that make a person or a person's existing state.

To get to the core of who we are, we must know how we came to be. The concept of who you are is deeply rooted in your subconscious mind. The value of your thoughts shape what you believe. Who you have come to be today is a direct result of the thoughts that have governed your mind.

I was raised to believe someone else's truth about life. This does not mean it was the truth, but it was *their* truth. Often, perception becomes reality. All my life I had been told I was "too dark to be loved or accepted." This message attached itself to my identity as if it were *true*. My response to this type of mental grooming was that I believed everything that happened to me happened because I wasn't good enough. I truly thought that life was supposed to be difficult for me because of the darker hue of my skin. The growth of self-hate within my mind and spirit grew rapidly. These untruths were planted in my mind since childhood and they governed my thinking into adulthood. I felt disconnected and felt the color of my skin was causing my demise. I had to find my true self even though I had no clue where to find her.

If I wanted to be free, I would have to re-evaluate who I was because who I had become was based on my family's and society's opinions and expectations of who I should be. Who I had become stemmed from the self-negating messages I received as a child. People I knew always told me, "Don't rock the boat, Sharon, stay beneath the radar and everything will be just fine," or "Do not draw attention to yourself. White people will only allow you to do so much," and "Don't trust no one."

The more I searched for the truth, the more I realized all the pieces of advice I had been given were fear-based. My family was teaching me what they had been taught. As I look back, that four-letter word (FEAR) had been detrimental to the mental and spiritual well- being of those around me. Individuals in my family were afraid of standing up and standing out and they taught me to be just as afraid as they were. They were giving me advice they believed would help me avoid disappointment, pain, failure, or false hopes. Not only was fear rooted within my family, but also, into the blueprint of most of my culture. I knew many around me who looked like me and hated themselves; therefore, they lacked the capacity to fully teach me to accept and love myself.

We must be mindful of the people, places, and things we allow ourselves, and our loved ones, to be exposed to. Take a mental note of the company you surround yourself with. Is their communication life giving to you and others? Knowingly, and unknowingly, we pass down ideologies, concepts, and beliefs to our families and those connected to us based on our personal experiences. For instance, you are sitting at the dinner table and you realize that you are behaving in the same way, and saying the same things, as your mother, father, or guardian. You told yourself you would never behave that way or say those words, but here you are. We find ourselves acting out the same negative behaviors because of normality, unconscious toxic thoughts and beliefs, and an unwillingness to accept truth and change. Change occurs by choosing a different path than we are accustomed to.

If our life experiences and circumstances originate from fear, pain, and hidden truths, we may inadvertently spread those ideas to our loved ones. It may be hard to make a mindset shift when all you do is recycle toxic thinking. A shifting of the mind, however, comes from change - a change of information, exposure to new knowledge, exposure to a new mindset, a change of environment, and a change of connections.

Examine who is in your friendship circle and who you allow to influence your life. Influence can be subtle. Have you ever been to visit a southern state or foreign country only to return home with a new accent? This is how easily we can be mentally influenced.

We can take on impressions, and oppressions, of others just by hanging out with them. The people, places, and things around you contribute to who you are. So, if you are not changing check your circle of acquaintances. In seeking the truth of who we are, we must examine who are our key influencers.

We should be aware of what and who we have allowed to shape our identity. Finding our true identity requires us to examine all aspects of **how and why** we have become who we are today. We are not our titles, positions or roles. We are who

God created us to be. Find that person who existed before the negativity showed up in your life.

You possess the power to change your world. You are a creator.

Who has been the most influential person in your life? Are they truly a health thinking y person? What life lessons have you learned from them?

_____

_____

_____

_____

_____

What messages have you received from family and society about who you should be? How have those closest to you influenced how you feel about yourself?

_____

_____

_____

_____

_____

How do you view and perceive yourself? Who are you?

_____

_____

_____

_____

_____

_____

How do you treat/view those who are not like you? Is privilege or bias part of your belief system? Is privilege who you are?

_____

_____

_____

_____

_____

_____

Don't be afraid to examine yourself. It can be the path to liberation.

Chapter Three
Believing the Lies

A lie is a false statement made with deliberate intent to deceive or mislead.

We fail to realize who we have become (our beliefs) is directly related to family and societal childhood experiences. To get to the root of our discourse and dissonance, we must travel back in time to when we were children. We must find the truth about some possible lies we were taught to believe were true. How we view others, how we think, and how we cope emotionally derive from the ideas our parents, guardians and society implanted in us. Be it good or bad. If your belief system has been created based on someone's faulty perspective, then here is where the work will begin to change those perspectives.

We must allow the truth into our hearts and minds if we truly want change. The lies we live with are affecting us and those around us negatively. It is up to us to free ourselves and others. We are responsible for our own growth, that growth collectively can change the world. If you grew up with privilege that has negatively impacted others, you have work to do.

Some of us were taught complete lies growing up just like the lies I was taught about my skin color throughout my childhood. As children, we tend to believe what we are told. If it is powerful and positive, we tend to believe it. If it is disempowering and toxic, we tend to believe it as well because it's what we were taught. We perceive the people around us based on our life experiences and what emotions we attach to those experiences. I was taught that being a black woman was wrong, less than, and hard. What were you taught about your race or other races? Write down the words that come to your mind.

Let's break the cycle of these lies. As a part of the process, I will always refer to my own childhood. You can do the same. I believe it is important to identify how you came to think the way you do based on your upbringing. My pain once crippled me because I was told, and believed, I was nothing. I *truly* believed I was nothing. I did not believe that I had value or purpose. I had to learn who I truly was and then I had to own the truth of my new knowledge. You must take ownership of the new information that you find, no matter how much you like or dislike your discoveries. What we are seeking is the truth. Are you ready to accept the truth? You may feel uncomfortable at first, but the truth will grant you true emotional freedom.

What family, cultural, and or societal beliefs would you like to question or challenge?

_____

_____

_____

_____

_____

Are there negative messages concerning race (your race or other races) that you were taught, but are afraid to examine? If so, what are they?

_____

_____

_____

_____

_____

Write down the internal mental messages (regarding your image/who you believe you are) you have received in your lifetime that may not be true.

_____

_____

_____

_____

Have you addressed these issues? Why? or Why not?

_____

_____

_____

_____

_____

Chapter Four

What Do You Say to Yourself?

I feel it is safe to say we have all experienced bouts of having not-so-positive thoughts of doubt, stress, worry and lack. As we move through life, feelings of insecurity can invade our minds. *"Who do you think you are?" "You will never accomplish this." "You are not smart enough." "You're not the right skin color." "You come from poverty and you will never make it out of poverty." "No one loves you."* These negative beliefs can replay over and over in our minds and they strangle the life out of us little by little if we allow them. I believed these lies and that led me to live an oppressive and depressing life. I never believed anything good would ever happen to me.

In the upcoming chapters, we will work through the issues and circumstances that create these types of unhealthy thoughts. The roots of who we are destined to become must be fed soul-nourishing ideas and truths. After we discover the truths of our negative thought life, we can then take ownership of what we find and allow truth to replace the negativity. I must emphasize the action of taking ownership. This may be a little cliché but when you know better, you can do better. We must take ownership of new thoughts to cultivate positive emotions and live a life of freedom. Taking ownership means that you will gather new information by reading or doing research concerning who you want to become. If you want to become a new thinker, do something different.

Take time every day to re-affirm yourself with positive words. While affirming and visualizing the new you, you will soon feel your emotions move in the same directions of your affirmations. It will happen! Let it be known, detoxing your thoughts is a major task. Anything in life worth having requires effort.

Are you up for the challenge? I hope so!

Just as coal miners dig until they find what they are looking for, you must be willing to excavate the unhealthy thoughts and beliefs in your mind.

Let's examine the many ways negative self-talk and thinking reveals itself to us.

Pessimistic Beliefs

Pessimism is seeing and believing the worst will happen. Do you believe the worst about another race? What do those thoughts imply? Write down the words that come to mind.

Think about that one co-worker everyone avoids because she or he never has a positive word to say. This type of person has adopted a pessimistic belief system and fails to consider alternative ways of thinking. You may have been this person once or you may be this person right now. Maybe you are not pessimistic in general but are you thinking pessimistic thoughts concerning another race. A pessimistic mindset creates an unhappy and unmotivated life because you never believe anything good is going to happen. If you think this way about other races you are part of the collective systemic problem as it pertains to bias and possibly racist views and action towards others. If you are the individual who always thinks the worst is going to happen, trust me when I tell you this: you need to figure out you think this way.

Having a core pessimistic belief system can stem from many things. It can be the result of having continuous tragic life events occur. This was me at one time. I had to look at my past life events that said, "Nothing good will ever happen in my life" and change this negative mental language to a positive language. I told myself that my past is my past and I will believe for a better today!

If you think of others negatively based on race, then you need to start congregating in places to experience the positive side of other cultures. Walk in their shoes mentally to grow empathy.

You may be thinking, "It isn't that easy," and I agree with you. It isn't. It takes courage to seek the truth, taking ownership of the truth without shame is going to be the uphill walk! *You can do this!*

Do you secretly try to move forward with the hopes of good but still believe that no good will happen? Do you create a good thought and then allow doubt to creep in with the next thought? This pessimistic paradox will keep you stuck in negativity. This is not helpful to you, but it can be changed if you take ownership of detoxing your thought life. Rest assured that it is never too late to make a change. Start believing and hoping again.

Desires of Perfectionism

Perfectionism is the refusal to accept any standard that is not *perfect.*   We can become our own worst enemy by having a strong desire for everything to be *perfect.* This is one-way negative self-talk occurs; it happens by telling yourself how perfect things need to be. The truth is: we must allow ourselves and others the right to make mistakes and have imperfections. Let's give the word mistake a better connotation. When most people hear or think of the word *mistake,* they automatically pair it with failure or a punitive definition. Let's consider the fact that making a *mistake* means you tried! Whoever told us that making a mistake leads to imperfection has been misled themselves. Keep these words in mind when you are thinking of your personal change. Don't be too hard on yourself; self-correction, self-discipline and self-accountability is necessary. Punishing ourselves is not helpful.

Dichotomous Thinking

Dichotomous thinking is one of the most toxic ways of thinking when used out of context or need. It means you operate with the mentality of "all or nothing" or "black or white." This type of thought process leaves no room for anything new or different to come forth. So, what do we do? I say own the fact that in this life there are a plethora of possibilities and different ways of doing things. Choose to see the silver lining on the dark clouds.

Dichotomous thinking does not allow for grey areas. But in this life, we all have grey experiences.

We think, we speak, and we create.

We create our worlds based on our thoughts (personally and collectively) whether they be subjective (personal thoughts) or objective (free from personal opinion). The things we allow ourselves to ponder impacts our decisions more than we may recognize and acknowledge. Are you pondering negative thoughts of yourself and others? Our thoughts are always being created and when we allow ourselves to rehearse scenarios of life that did not work out in our favor without resolution, we rob ourselves of feeling the present moment's joy. We allow our greatest creative abilities to be tainted because we do not understand the importance of mastering our thought life. *Proverbs 23:7 (KJV)* says, *"As man a thinketh in his heart, so is he."* If our thoughts create what manifests in the physical, why do we not spend more time cultivating, purifying, healing and maturing the way we think? Healing will be lost if you do not stop the negative thoughts.

We must begin to visualize ourselves living a new life. Visualize yourself doing the things you want to do but are too afraid to do. I would sit and see myself in healthy and loving relationships going as far as visualizing the sun in the sky and the wind blowing the leaves down the street as I am walking with loved ones that respected me and supported me. Visualize the world around you fee of bias and racism. I know that is a tall order, but we must start somewhere. Allow yourself the joy of dreaming.

I believe our own mental inhibitions interrupt our healthy thoughts. I believe we can redirect our lives by redirecting our thoughts. We must seek to attain new knowledge and gain an understanding of ourselves and others to live out our fullest potential. The best part about living is knowing that each day is new!

In life, I believe the Creator gives us clues to follow - some call it intuition or discernment - or your 'gut feeling.' These clues are given to guide us to the right path of travel. If the negative thoughts you have resound louder than your intuition, discernment, and your 'gut feeling', you may not be able to understand what God is trying to show you. You won't trust your nudgings or what you are 'hearing' through your intuition. If we are still with our thoughts, the Creator has a way of showing us what we really need to work on- spiritually, physically and mentally.

In the next few chapters we will look at some of the specific emotions and issues that plague many lives. Your task will be to identify how you feel concerning these issues. In doing so, your work will begin. Together, we can get started with detoxing our thoughts. Happy thoughts lead to a happy life.

Write down what you say to yourself.

_____

_____

_____

In what ways do you think negatively about other cultures? Write down the words that come to mind. (subhuman, disgusting, bad, no good)

_____

_____

_____

How do you feel when these toxic thoughts are present? (fearful subservient, less than, privileged, powerless, better than)

_____

_____

_____

What purpose do these negative thoughts serve?

_____

_____

_____

_____

_____

Write down a plan to replace negative thoughts. (research, counseling)
What behaviors will you need to change?

_____

_____

_____

_____

_____

_____

_____

_____

_____

_____

_____

_____

_____

_____

_____

_____

Chapter Five

Fear of Failing

Failure is the state or condition of not meeting a desirable or intended objective. It is also viewed as the opposite of success.

The fear of failure is a feeling most of us have at various points in our lives. When we think of failure, we think doom and defeat. For example, if I stumbled over my words, or I forgot to mention something in a meeting, I would beat myself up afterwards. Fear of failure prevented me from making decisions. I did not want to make a decision that held the possibility of failure. For quite some time, I did not do *anything* that placed me outside of my comfort zone; I thought I was protecting myself from the risk of failure. However, this was simply not the case. If I failed at anything, it was judgement day and I was the judge.

Allowing fear to stop us in any capacity will stunt mental and spiritual growth and prohibit us from moving past fearful thoughts. We need to be open to new thoughts that will allow us to overcome the fear of failure. Let's face it, it's time to rid our minds and spirits of fear because on the other side of fear is always victory.

The process of overcoming fear may not feel good. However, anytime you go where fear tells you not to go you have won! *What does failure look like to you?* For me, failure walked hand in hand with punishment. I did not really have to do anything to be punished as a child because I lived in a punitive household; we were punished for any and everything. I was not going to take the chance of doing something wrong, just to get into more trouble. Because of this, I thought that it was not okay to make a mistake – ever. I would not do anything outside of my normal routine because I did not want to fail. My mind was on autopilot, always thinking the worst. I knew not to place myself in situations that could potentially lead to failure out of the fear of punishment. Growing up in a punitive based household can create an internalized negative core belief that says, "If I am wrong or make a mistake I must pay." I thought negative consequences would always be the result of failing.

I had to figure out, through self-questioning, why I was so critical and judgmental of myself and, unknowingly, punishing myself for making mistakes. What I found out was that even though the 'punishers' were physically gone from my life; their voices were not. I kept those old beliefs and they played in my mind any time the fear of failure would show up. I did not know how to change the toxic core thoughts and beliefs that played on autopilot in my mind, so I became my own 'punisher.' I used to be my own worst critic but now I know how to love myself past my failures.

Do you tend to be hard on yourself? Identify why?

_____

_____

_____

_____

_____

The idea of failure made me unsure about who I was as a person. The value I held for myself was based on what I did right or wrong. Nothing else. I did not hold the belief that I could be *good* and *fail*. This thought and belief just did not exist in my mind or life experiences. I did not believe that I was deserving of everything good in life. The feelings I experienced when I failed were almost unbearable, so I tried my hardest to stay away from any person or experience that made me feel this way. I had to become aware that I was stockpiling feelings of self-hatred and criticism of self. As

31

soon as I became conscious of my self-critic and self-hate, I was able to begin to learn how to love myself. Now I know how to love me, and you can learn to love you as well.

Shame

Shame is the result of feeling deep humiliation, deep inadequacy, inferiority, or deep self-loathing. Shame can be the result of you feeling that you believe you're flawed.

The feeling of shame is often followed by embarrassment. Feelings of shame makes us want to seclude ourselves from anyone who can judge us. My experience with feelings of shame held me hostage for quite some time. I refused to talk in front of large groups of people because I was afraid of *knowing* what they thought about me. I did not put myself in any situations where people could judge me.

As a child or even as an adult, can you recall feeling this way? How has it affected your sense of freedom and self-expression?

_____

_____

_____

_____

I am not sure when I realized it, but I started to notice that, as an adult, I was the one shaming myself the most, not others. Yes, as a child, my family and society had much to do with my negative perceptions of life. But as an adult, I was holding on to every negative idea I had experienced as a child. Any time someone would ask me to speak, I became deathly afraid because I did not want to make a mistake or look foolish. I did not want to feel shame ever again, so I allowed my negative thoughts to keep me away from many great experiences.

I was taught that God was going to 'get' me if I sinned. I felt tremendous shame for doing anything wrong, so I stayed away from the church as well, fearing the wrath of God. I know now what I was taught was not the truth. However, my thought life needed to be transformed. It took time for my new beliefs to become truth. I had to learn to put shame in its place by completely reprogramming my mind to speak positive words of affirmations into my spirit. I speak these words over my life:

I am not a failure

I am not ashamed

 I am capable

The result of failure is not punishment.

Tools

When the old thoughts try to come up again, we will "control-alt-delete" them.

Control - I will Control thoughts that I allow into my mind. (Breath In)

Alt - I will Stop all negative and toxic thoughts. (Exhale)

Delete - I will Replace all negative/toxic thoughts with positive, life-giving thoughts (Breath In)

Remember, affirmations along with visualization makes reality! Affirm yourself and see yourself as the affirmation.

I also forgave those, including myself, who made me feel deep shame. I could forgive once I became aware that the shameful messages from my past have no power over me today. I did the work to change my thoughts and beliefs.

Where does your fear of failing come from? Do you believe failing is wrong?

_____

_____

_____

_____

Who told you to be afraid of failing and or making mistakes?

_____

_____

_____

_____

How has shame caused you to miss opportunities?

_____

_____

_____

_____

_____

_____

Chapter Six
Fear of Success

I have accomplished so many things in my life but at one point, I could not seem to truly feel the joy of my accomplishments. I had written a book, co-authored a best-selling book, and got clean and sober, yet I didn't feel like I was successful. I wanted to enjoy my success when my first book was published but I was riddled with anxieties. I thought: *What if no one reads it or what if no one likes it?* The power of "what if" had me paralyzed. I would go for walks and cry out to asking the Creator *"Why can't I enjoy anything?"*

I had conquered major barriers in my life, and I should have been happy with myself, yet, for some reason I was not. I had to get to the point where I could say, "I am a published author and I am free of drugs," and actually enjoy the moment. I had to begin working towards accepting the fact that I have weaknesses and one of those weaknesses was fear.

I was stuck in a stale mindset - a mindset that was cultivated in me since childhood. I felt like I was not good enough because the thought, "I don't deserve anything," was embedded in my belief system. I believed if I did something good, I should be grateful not excited for the opportunity because it may not last and something bad was going to ruin it. I never felt worthy enough to enjoy receiving opportunities. My constant undeserving mentality plagued everything I did. When bad things happened, I believed I deserved them. Every time I would do something good, it didn't hold value. I wasn't taught that I was valuable. All my life society and family taught me that my skin color made me less than.

Nothing that I could do was ever good enough for me. I didn't really believe I was good enough to succeed nor did I believe I was deserving of the compliments that affirmed my successes. When someone would give me a compliment, I would feel uncomfortable receiving it. You see compliments were not familiar to me. I did not like the way compliments made me feel, but I smiled and politely said "thank you." I feared being looked at as "successful" because I didn't believe I was. I would get mad because I wanted to really enjoy my life! I never wanted to gloat, but I did want to feel like what I was doing was "okay."

You see, I feared *both* failure and success. I felt paralyzed in my life and I needed to learn to accept my accomplishment and myself. I began to recite this affirmation daily:

I am deserving of all the good life offers. I am deserving.

We all have fears. W*hy do we allow them to stop us from believing in our dreams*? We fear success for many reasons; we don't believe it will ever happen, we don't believe we are deserving of success, we treat it like a negative, heavy responsibility, or we don't believe we can make it happen. For a multitude of reasons, we do not allow ourselves the right to think we can achieve certain things in life. Perhaps it is because we are afraid to feel disappointment if we do not achieve what we desire. We sometimes want things but are not willing to put in the work to attain those wants because we do not believe we can sustain them. When obstacles come, we get discouraged and we want to quit. We don't look for the path to change that same obstacle into an opportunity to grow. Start defying the urge to quit! You deserve success and you can own it. See yourself reaching your goals and dreams and imagine how it will feel. Are your dreams worth the hard work and efforts you will put forth to bring them to fruition? Yes, they are!

Start giving yourself credit throughout your day for both major and minor successes. Stop comparing yourself to others and realize who you are. You are worth it! Accept your greatness! Focus on your strengths to improve your weaknesses. When you finish a task, acknowledge the work you have done to get the task completed.

You deserve your own praise!

If you're an intense self-critic, stop being your own *worst* critic. There is always room for improvement in all we do. Realize it is ok not to know everything. There is purpose in learning opportunities. If you make a mistake, think of it as a learning moment, not a time of belabored, self-crucifixion. Learn from it and continue to move forward. Breathe, relax and enjoy the ride to success.

Are you sabotaging your own success? Why?

_____

_____

_____

_____

_____

What critical and judgmental thoughts do you have of yourself?

_____

_____

_____

_____

_____

_____

_____

_____

GIVE YOURSELF A BREAK. BE NICE TO YOU.

Chapter Seven

Abandonment & Rejection

Abandonment is the act of abandoning or being abandoned; to leave completely and finally, forsake utterly, to give up; to discontinue, and or to withdraw from.

I remember the first time I felt abandoned because it hurt so badly. I told myself I would never feel that way again. The triggers of abandonment can be vast and can look different for everyone. I found that my trigger for feeling this type of pain was watching people leave my life. It seemed as if no matter what I did, people would come in and out of my life with no warning. I would spend so much time and energy trying to analyze why those relationships never worked out. With each end, I would obsess over possible reasons why. I would analyze the relationship from beginning to end and wonder, *What on earth did I do to these individuals to make them not want me anymore?*

Do you remember the first time you felt abandoned? My over-analyzation only resulted in me ripping my self-esteem to pieces.

I would ask myself the same questions repeatedly: *What did I do wrong? Why don't they like me? Why don't I have many friends like everyone else?*

I would tell myself that I should change who I was so people would like me more and I could make them want to stay with me. I went on a people pleasing journey and I changed aspects of my life in attempts to make others more comfortable. I gave up me for them. My emotions where on autopilot, they told me what to do and I did it. My mission was to find out what was wrong with me. This wore on my *soul* and caused me to spiral into emotional turmoil.

What was wrong with me? I started to wonder if I unintentionally harmed those who left me but, I later found out some of the reasons people left me had nothing to do with me. My abandonment issues were so deeply rooted in my psyche that I did not realize that it was ok for people to leave me. I had internalized multiple fallacies that told me if someone leaves me it is because something must be wrong with me. I was allowing all the wrong people into my life out of fear of being abandoned and alone. **I did not want to be alone.**

Throughout my childhood, I was always made to feel like the outsider. I spent a lot of time alone and I did not like that feeling, I wanted to be wanted. I didn't get the nurturing as a child to feel secure in this world, so I searched for this feeling on my own. However, because of my limited teaching of love and acceptance, I attracted and connected all the wrong individuals.

To nurture is the process of caring for and encouraging the development and growth of someone. Nurturing is a very important part of a child's development. When there is a lack of nurture, children are led to feel unwanted and unloved. Not only did I feel this way as a child, but I carried those emotions and memories of abandonment into my adult life. Feeling alone equaled abandonment for me. The thought of being alone and abandoned was too much, so I accepted into my life any and everyone who showed me attention. I was so needy for acceptance that I *craved* to be around anyone who would give me positive or negative attention. This craving led me to be influenced by individuals who had not overcome their own negative thinking and toxic behaviors.

Identifying these negative feelings will help you to begin to pinpoint where negative patterns began and understand what's behind certain patterns of behavior or poor decision-making. We should get to a point where we realize it is not always a bad thing when certain people leave our lives. People come and people go- it is a natural occurrence. For some, coping with the loss of one person means finding three other people to take their place. Learning to acknowledge how you feel instead of using people, places or things to cover your feelings is imperative for change. The problem arises when unresolved issues of abandonment resurface, and we have no tools to deal with the pain we are experiencing.

I had to realize the decisions of others to leave was their decision to make. This was a hard lesson for me to learn. I overlooked the signs that showed me that some of the people I allowed into my space were not deserving of me or my time. For example, I ignored toxic behavior, accepted little white lies, and tolerated disrespect. It was so important for me to be accepted that I simply acted as if these unhealthy behaviors were not important. What I was really doing was creating more pain for myself because I did not release dysfunctional individuals.

Do you feel as if your childhood lacked nurturing moments? How does this make you feel? How has this impacted your life?

_____

_____

_____

_____

_____

What mindsets have you cultivated because of abandonment?

_____

_____

_____

_____

_____

Who made you feel alone and unwanted? Have you forgiven them?

_____

_____

_____

_____

Rejection

To reject means to dismiss as inadequate and not acceptable.

In my first book, *Chronicles of Pain: Leaving the Pain of the Past Behind* I wrote, "I can still feel the rejection of others, and this feeling of rejection shaped my life in a terrible way." My family, love interests and friends rejected me. This constant rejection made me feel as if no one loved me. This also gave me the belief that I was not good enough for anyone to love. I concluded that I was unlovable and lived my life as such. I lived with feelings of rejection and I fought to stay in relationships with individuals who rejected me because rejection was all I knew. Yes, I fought for the toxic familiar feelings of rejection as painful as they were. I used to cry myself to sleep wondering, *"Will anyone every just love me?"*

The more I desired change, the more I started recognizing a few things. The first thought I embraced was the fact that the Creator loved me and if no one else accepted me, the Creator accepted me. Then I needed to accept me for me; I learned to accept me. This caused me to believe that my life is no longer determined by someone else's approval or want of me. I am a divine creation, wanted and needed by love, for love and for a purpose. I am not a reject. We are worth more than what our negative false core beliefs tell us. We can give and receive love and respect without settling for toxic and dysfunctional relationships. We must believe and love ourselves enough to reject the things that do not empower us to believe in the good of who we are.

Have you experienced moments where you felt like you had no one?

_____

_____

_____

What do you do when you feel like no one is there to support you?

_____

_____

_____

How do you accept you? YOU ARE NOT A REJECT. Write affirmations that support you.

_____

_____

_____

Feel What You Feel

Identify the times in your life when you felt abandoned and alone, this will help you become aware of past hurts and move away from them. Becoming aware of feelings of abandonment can cause one to feel bad just as detoxing from negative thoughts and emotions will cause some uneasy feelings to arise. Allow yourself to feel what you feel and then apply your new truth (scriptures/affirmations) to your situation to move past those emotions. Don't stay stuck. Its ok to get down, but don't stay stuck there. We can arrive at an awareness that feeling alone/abandoned and actually being alone/abandoned are two different perceptions. The next few questions will help lead you to uncovering your behavior patterns.

Are you afraid to be alone? Why? When you feel alone what do you do?

_____

_____

_____

_____

_____

Are you chasing a familiar toxic feeling?

_____

_____

_____

_____

_____

Do you recognize a dysfunctional cycle in your relationships?

_____

_____

_____

_____

Why is it not ok for people to leave your life?

_____

_____

_____

_____

_____

Chapter Eight
The Anger Inside

Anger is defined as wrath. An intense emotional response.

Do you anger easily?
You must search for the root of your anger. However, it will take some honesty and ownership of the truth on your behalf. *Are you ready?*

Anger is one of the most unpleasant of all emotions. Anger is natural and helps us respond to life's situations. However, when anger is out of control it causes much harm - not only to us, but also to those around us. I grew up in an African American household and my skin had the **darkest tone in** my family. I was told that because I was the darkest, I would have to do the most work and I was treated differently than my siblings. Now, I was mad because I did not look like them and I felt like I was worth less than them because of the hue of my skin. The rest of my family had "high yellow" skin tones. My stepfather taught me to believe that they were superior because of their skin tone. I felt like an outcast.

At the same time, we lived in a city called White Center (literally) and most of all our neighbors were Caucasian. We would wake up to see "KKK" spray painted on our bright yellow house and this made me angry. I was taught to fear white people because of the Ku Klux Klan (white supremacy group), but little did I know I was also taught to fear certain Black people as well. I learned that the lighter your skin tone was the more superior you were treated. Lighter was better and darker was inferior. I was confused and frustrated at a very young age. I had no clue where I fit in the grand scheme of things. The rage I felt because I didn't fit in was turned inward. I didn't fit anywhere. I was not accepted at home or in my community. I was experiencing an ultimate case of identity crisis. I stayed mad all the time but had no idea why. I went to extreme measures to fit in with my peers and family. My anger was rooted in this crisis.

The messages my young mind received were not okay. I could never express this as a child because I didn't think anyone would believe me. I was told not to trust white people, but I couldn't verbalize my mistrust of my own race either. So, I stayed silently mad for a very long time and my anger grew worse and worse. It grew to the point where I was always fighting. I fought hard as a child, and when I became an adult, I fought anyone over anything. People kept asking me why I was always so angry, but I never knew how to answer. "What goes on in this house, stays in this house," my family told me. So, when asked, I kept my mouth shut.

One day I got tired of being angry all the time and I decided to look at my pain and anger for what it was. I knew my angry outburst no longer needed to get the best of me. I started the process of forgiving those people who hurt me, and I replaced anger with love
- one experience at a time. This time, I fought to retrain my mind and emotions to let go of what was. I searched my mind to locate the negative recordings of the bad things people said to me over the years, so I could delete them. I even worked hard to let go of my negative thoughts towards myself. In ridding myself of those thoughts, I replaced them with the word of God and factual positive affirmations. With guidance from the Creator and the help of others, I started to accept and love me.

My forgiveness declaration went something like this: *I will no longer harbor hatred for others regardless of the reason. I will*

accept the fact that what happened to me was painful, but I have
no need of the pain and anger any longer. I choose to deal with
the pain that I feel and move away from it.

In addition to forgiving yourself, *who do you need to forgive and*
release for causing you pain? I did not choose to get hurt but I
have chosen not to allow the hurt from my past to dictate my
future. When my past pain tries to sneak back into my life, I tell
it exactly where it can go. We must all learn to be the conductor
of our thoughts. If we choose not to intentionally direct our
thoughts, then we leave the negative programmed thoughts and
toxic core beliefs to run our lives.

Are you defensive? Give some examples of how and why?

_____

_____

_____

_____

_____

_____

_____

Are most of your responses made in anger or with a mean-nature? If so, what do you believe is causing your anger?

_____

_____

_____

_____

_____

Chapter Nine

Anxieties Equal Uncertainties

Anxiety is a feeling of worry, nervousness, or unease, typically about an imminent event or something with an uncertain outcome.

I used to wonder why I always felt a feeling of uneasiness. A sense of overwhelming sadness would often come over me and fear would rise in my chest sending my heart into working overtime. I had no control over these sensations when they started. Many times, I would end up in the emergency room or in my doctor's office. I was under medical care so much that I believe I could have hooked up the EKG machine myself. Sometimes, I could see the look of worry written over the faces of my children because they had no idea what was wrong with their mom. I was a wreck!

I hired a therapist who informed me of my issue. I was having anxiety attacks and I never knew it. I was told my problem was in my mind and that my body was reacting to what my mind and thoughts were telling it to do. This confused me so I asked for clarification. She took me back to my past. I remember living in uncertainty and fear even as a child. I started to remember how I would feel when my step-dad would come home night after night drunk. We would all feel scared. As a child, I never knew how strong the impact of these experiences would be in my adult life. On my road to healing, I discovered just how much my feelings of anxiety and uncertainty from my childhood tainted my adult happiness. When I felt fear or nervousness my mind would subconsciously catapult me into a place of my past. My body would immediately go into "fight or flight" mode-which is a psychological response to a perceived harmful event, attack, and or threat of survival. I know it sounds crazy, but it is real! I would feel fear and then my mind's perception would kick into overdrive because it perceived more danger than was currently taking place. ONE of many ways to overcome anxiety is to find out what thoughts are triggering the attacks.

Also, during my time working with a therapist, I learned I was gravitating toward the toxic thoughts and emotions that *caused* my anxiety attacks because of their familiar feeling. People like "the familiar" and gravitate towards things or individuals that are familiar even if those things and people are toxic. Though this may seem strange, having a negative life is what felt comfortable to me.

I gravitated towards relationships that kept me feeling uncertain. The anxiety I suffered due to uncertainty was ruining my life, but I did not know it. The uncertainty I felt kept me guessing and fearing everything. I never allowed myself time to relax and allow things to be ok. My common sense told me to stay away from anything that gave me bad feelings, but on the other hand, I felt comfortable with a sense of dis-ease. For example, I would be having a great day but would feel like something was missing. The thing I was missing was the uncertainty! I wasn't ok with everything being good because that would be too good to be true. It's crazy thinking back how I sabotaged my own happiness because of a toxic familiar feeling.

My thought processes were in total contradiction of one another causing my anxiety to spiral out of control. My mind was constantly in battle and this battle fueled my anxiety daily. For example, if someone dependable and reliable came into my life, I pulled away from them. Why? Because my mind viewed them as unfamiliar, so it rejected the sense of reliability that should have given me a sense of stability. I wanted stability, but I never experienced it, so I rejected it. The only thing I could remember was the chaos and the calamity of my life. Happy times were few and far between per my memory. I gravitated towards those individuals who were just as unstable as I. Both my romantic relationships and platonic friendships suffered because of this.

When anxiety starts manifesting in my body, I take a few moments to figure out what is causing it. I ask myself: *What am I feeling? Is this feeling due to my present situation or past situation? Does this experience I am having remind me of a past trauma? Does this situation validate the emotion my body is wanting to produce?*

Asking myself these questions helped me to identify the truth about my circumstances and aided me in tapping into my emotions. It is important to identify what it is you are feeling so you can gain control over your mind and body.

Our thoughts are very powerful, and they create our realities. We cannot allow random thoughts to roam around in our minds; we must recognize and stop negative thoughts and emotions from taking over. For most people, including me, there's often not much thought given to the roots of our thoughts. Now that I know better, I do better! I want to live a life free from the oppression of anxiety, uncertainty, and instability. There is a scripture in the bible that I hold dear and it helps me to calm down and recognize that whatever is happening around me *must* pass. This scripture is, "And we know that God causes everything to work together for the good of those who love God and are called according to his purpose." *Romans NLT 8:28*. For me this scripture kills anxiety because it tells me it doesn't matter how bad things look, it will all work out for my good. Through it all, my relationship with God has taught me how to face life head on.

Phobias

Phobias can cause anxiety symptoms; it is a strong irrational fear of something that poses no real threat.

Phobias can be devastating to say the least! I personally know what affect phobia have on the mind. They can control your life and it will if you allow it! The best way overcome phobias is to face them! The very thing we are afraid of is the very thing that holds the power to unlocking our freedom. Yes, the thought of facing your biggest fear may seem horrifying but which is better confronting them or staying stuck? Phobias come in many forms. When we have phobias, we trust our emotions over our realities, and this stops our forward motion in life.

My fears included exposure, confinement, and doing anything outside of my normal routine. The more I listened to my negative thoughts, the greater the toxic reaction in my body evolved. I would start to get hot and then my heart would begin to race and before I knew it, I just wanted out of the situation! I would go out to eat at restaurants with friends and order the same old things because I was afraid of having an allergic reaction to foods that I had not consumed before. I would go through this whole mental process: *Okay that looks good and it looks like it tastes wonderful! I think I'll try it...Well, maybe not. It may have something in it that could close my throat up and kill me!* After about two minutes of this type of negative self- talk, I had fully convinced myself to stay the course that I knew was safe.

Then there was the fear of exposure - I did not want anyone to see me. I loved to stay behind the scenes and had no desire to be in the spotlight. I remember writing my first book. After I gave it to the publisher, I lost it! I started to have anxiety attacks - my blood pressure was higher than normal, and I found myself back in the hospital. I thought I was over having these attacks, but the exposure triggered my un-examined and un-treated fears.

I decided to meditate and ask the Creator to reveal many things from my past. I began reading through my old journals and noticed my pattern of dysfunctional behaviors. I kept writing about how I should not talk or tell anyone about what happens at home. As an addict, I never let anyone see me use drugs because they could not prove you where an addict unless they saw you using - everything else was simply speculation. I noticed another pattern, the pattern of secrets

I wrote my first book because I wanted to help others who were drug addicted, abused and afraid to come out of that lifestyle. I thought I truly did not care if anyone heard my story, however, I never knew how much unveiling these things about myself openly would affect how I felt about the secrets I kept. I had never dealt with my life's secrets. Yes, I was willing to tell the story, but I had not yet recognized how my secrecy reinforced a phobia of exposure.

Another fear was the fear of being confined. I absolutely hated for anyone to try to hold me down. I also hated to get into elevators or planes. My kids and I used to wrestle, and I would literally go nuts when they would try to hold me down as if we were not playing. My children did not understand my reactions and neither did I. Being held against your will is far from a pleasant experience. One of my excs would hold me down against my will and that feeling of being restrained was a horrible memory for me. He ruled me with fear and my way of dealing with it was to not think about what he said but just do it. I had no idea that stuffing emotions would haunt me later on in life.

I remember having an anxiety episode on **an airplane** flight once. After not flying much in the past, I ended up having to take a flight out of state. As soon as I stepped on the plane, I freaked out! I had the most horrible time trying to calm myself down; and after that flight I vowed never to fly again. I forgot I had to get back home.

I did not face my fear of confinement until I had to make a trip to St. Louis to visit family and an anxiety attack surfaced again. My cousin wanted to take me to see the historic arch and I was excited to see it - only I did not know you could go inside the arch. To get to the top, which was 630 feet in the air, we had to ride in a small tram. I told her *we* would not be making that trip anytime soon. She was sweetly persistent in urging me to join her, so I finally caved. At the ticket counter, there was a life size replica of the tram that took you to the top and when I saw it, I was

66

determined that I would not get in it. I sat in this replica of an egg-shaped vehicle, which tightly seated about five people. I hated it! My cousin was calm. She asked me what I was afraid of and I told her being confined and not being able to get out if something went wrong. She assured me nothing bad would happen. So, off we went.

I made the mistake of opening my eyes about a minute from the top. I started to freak out, but I managed to calm myself down by telling myself that what I was afraid of was not rational to my current experience and that I would be ok. When I got out, I wanted to cry. I felt so many emotions including anger because my fear was trying to stop me from a great experience. I was happy that my fear was not real. In that moment reality hit. I was deeply afraid of re-living my past.

I also found out that control played a role in my fears. I told myself I would never place myself in positions that I could not control. Because of my past experiences with domestic violence, I vowed that no one would ever be able to control me again. I had to deal with these fears and let them know they were not necessary any longer. The fear was showing up as a defense mechanism to protect me. However, these fears were not warranted for my present-day situation. Fear can only stop you if you allow it. We can move forward in the face of fear to overcome it.

What are you avoiding because of fear?

_____

_____

_____

_____

_____

YOU ARE MORE THAN YOUR FEARS.

ON THE OTHER SIDE OF FEAR IS WHERE YOUR PASSION AND PURPOSE RESIDES. BECOME FEARLESS!

Write about experiences where you have ignored your emotions.

_____

_____

_____

_____

Chapter Ten
Is Emotional Pain an Addiction?

Life's roadblocks, such as continuous failed relationships and unexpected circumstances, can keep us from advancing. However, emotional pain can serve as a path to greater self-awareness, growth, learning and clarity if you're willing to uncover the patterns you may have created. When I decided to take a look at the painful events of my life, it allowed me to gain an understanding of how I was thinking. As I began to write down the patterns of my thoughts, it became apparent to me WHO I really was as a thinking human. I found out that because of my numerous experiences with pain and trauma, I had become emotionally dependent on the feelings of pain (pain addiction). Just like any other addiction, you get used to feeling a certain way. If you do not feel it, you miss it - you crave it.

I wanted to be loved and that was my goal. I would meet some really nice guys but because there was no pain involved, I ran from those relationships. I didn't know it then, but I know it now. What I was searching for was that familiar feeling of pain. Could this be the reason why some of us have a hard time letting go of painful memories and the emotions associated with them? Are we even aware that pain can become a habit-forming craving? We all want to feel love but for some individuals, pain is what is most familiar. So, are you really searching for love? Or pain? People sometimes unknowingly seek a toxic emotional state and are unaware of it. If all one knows is hurt, then hurt is what they will seek.

Can you identify your own toxic patterns of being drawn to pain?

_____

_____

_____

_____

_____

What is your normal/familiar emotion or feeling?

_____

_____

_____

_____

_____

I believe it is easier to change how we look at pain if we apply love and forgiveness for ourselves as well as others. I believe God gives us the power to forgive ourselves and others. Love unlocks the door for our change and forgiveness creates a path back to love.

We can change our response to pain. However, it will take consistent work. This does not mean that hurt will not occur, but it does mean there is a possibility we can view the pain through new lenses. Become cognizant of your thought life. What and who are those thoughts manifesting in your life? If your life is filled with drama and pain take a deeper look at your thought life, it may be part of the problem.

The pain can cease in time if we allow it to. The reality is hurt people do hurt people. Whether you realize it or not, you could unintentionally be spreading pain to others. You should take note of your conduct and behavior you exhibit because of the pain you have endured. For example, I discovered my family spread pain around as if it was love. The way they treated each other caused hurt not love. This behavior was taught to them and in return they inflicted the same painful behaviors onto others. People can only give what they possess and nothing more. So, if someone in your life is only giving hurt and mistrust, that's all they have to give. Stop looking to get something they are not giving. Changing the negative way we process and respond to pain is imperative to changing our thought life.

Can you identify times in your life where you have gravitated towards individuals that cause pain?

As human beings, we think of pain as something that we should not have to feel. For those of us who have made portions of our life's mission not to feel pain, we must unlearn this concept. Pain is a part of life. Running and hiding from pain is not the answer. Trying to hide from the possibility of encountering pain means that you're avoiding life and fully living. In all actuality, not dealing with your junk prolongs the healing process.

Failure to manage the effects of emotional pain can cause other negative effects to surface in other areas of your life, such as your health and relationships. You may try to convince yourself that the pain of an experience is not affecting you. Pain that isn't addressed, constructively, can turn into anxiety, fear, insecurities, shame, sadness, and even depression. These feelings can show up when we repeatedly refuse to deal with our pain. Our bodies have a way of sending signals that let us know something is not right.

Memory

Memory is a storehouse of experiences and it serves us in many ways. Our memories allow us to recall things from our past and confront things in our present. It bridges the gap between what was and what is. The way we respond and react to life's situations is based primarily on the information that has been etched into our minds.

We all have memories we have tried to forget - especially those that try to plague our minds. Some of these memories we have blocked out and we refuse to allow them to resurface, but eventually memory will remind us of the pain we tried to stuff and hide.

We may have chosen not to "deal" with past painful life experiences; in that case, we may have inadvertently left a few mental *wounds* untreated. It hurts us to uncover painful feelings, but it is necessary if we really want to extricate ourselves from dwelling in the past.

Is emotional pain an addiction for you? Are you drawn to drama?

Seek professional help if these memories are too painful to deal with on your own.

Chapter Eleven
Disease by Thoughts

It is a fact that many autoimmune diseases and illness are closely linked to stress. The medical society has diagnosed me with Lupus. They informed me that I should monitor my stress levels and the foods I eat. At the time of my diagnosis, the information I received about stress and autoimmune disease was not clear; I gave no thought to underlying stressors. However, my lack of awareness of my unhealed emotional issues, does not mean they didn't exist. Underlying stressors showed up in my physical health exams. My physical and emotional health was on a roller coaster. It nearly drove me insane because I couldn't figure out what was wrong. I did not know that my past *emotional* pain had become a *physical* issue.

I finally took notice and accepted the fact that my past pain contributed to my toxic thought process, which aided in severe Lupus flares. Days after I would engage in conflict with another person, I would get dangerously sick. I was experiencing a delayed physical response to emotional stress. So, I began to think, if I am sick from a minor conflict how much of this sickness was based on unresolved conflict? I thought about all the emotions I felt from past conflicts-hurts, anger, rejection, shame, abuse, trauma and abandonment. My unresolved issues had to be dealt with because they were manifesting negatively in my physical body.

Furthermore, my reactions to familiar toxic emotions needed a new route of travel. I needed to change how I was responding to what I was feeling. What I needed to do was examine myself to see if I was reacting to conflict from my *past* or to conflict in my *present.* After much research and counseling, I began to learn how to respond differently to life in general. When I began to take ownership of the fact that my extreme range of emotions was not warranted, I learned to deal with my pain. Acknowledging my past hurts was what I did to begin my physical healing journey. As my thoughts were changing, my physical life began to follow suit.

I spoke this affirmation over my body: *I love you, and I will no longer harbor negative emotions that are damaging you.* Applying the word of God to my painful past helped me heal. I believe God Created us in His image. God created the body to be disease free, not sick or sickly. That means we should be healthy. Genesis 1:27 (NIV) God created man in his own image…

What unresolved conflict are you ignoring?

_____

_____

_____

_____

_____

It is time to make amends and move forward with life? Who do you need to make amends with? Is it yourself?

_____

_____

_____

_____

_____

_____

_____

_____

Chapter Twelve
Doubt the Doubt

Whenever a thought of doubt creeps into your mind, don't just believe it - question it! Ask that thought where did it come from and why does it exist? Living afraid and scared of making achievements in life is no way to live. We should learn to doubt the doubt! Doubt the negative toxic thoughts you have and replace those thoughts with healthy new thoughts. Cut off the "blood flow" to toxic people and situations. In other words, stay away from toxicity if possible. The reality is, we will incur negative and toxic people throughout our lives. Change your circle of friends and those who influence you if they do not affirm and push you forward to your destiny. When you begin mastering removing your own unhealthy ways of thinking, you can help others do the same.

Now it is not enough to just recite scriptures and affirmations about your thoughts and your circumstances, you must take ownership of new healthy thoughts to see real lasting change in your thought life. YOU MUST BELIEVE! I learned that to reconstruct my mind I first had to be an active participant in spending quiet time with my Creator. Make it a goal to spend quiet time meditating early in your day before the hustle and bustle of life seeps in. The way you start your day will determine how your day goes. When you awake in the morning don't allow the negativity of yesterday to seep in. Start with gratitude and thanksgiving first thing in the morning. Begin our day by affirming all that is good about you and then state your expectations for the day.

Doubt the thought that you can't make it. Doubt the thought that says, "In this life you will be a failure." Doubt the negative old messages from your past. Doubt fear, shame, anxiety, failure, fear of success and doubt every negative toxic word that has been spoken over your life! Doubt the thought that you will not ever be happy or in love with you. You are enough for you and you are more than enough for someone else. You must believe you are deserving of the best and that you will become the best version of yourself. Never stop searching for the truth. Read, research and read again until you are satisfied with the truth. You should know why you think a certain thought. "I don't know" is no longer an acceptable answer. We should no longer allow random thoughts to run rapid in our minds.

Acknowledging a new truth will require a willingness to accept the fact that what you may know, may not be true.

Chapter Thirteen
Dream Again

Dreams deferred can feel like someone is ripping all hope and faith away from you if you allow the process to detour your hope and faith. A dream deferred can keep you hoping and doubting at the same time. The patience and faith that must accompany dreaming requires persistence.

DO YOU HAVE PATIENCE, I ASK?

Do you have the patience and determination to sustain the doubt that would come to kill every unfulfilled dream that lays dormant in your mind? You know those dreams that you told God about, and now you have made excuses for the reality that they have not yet come to pass. What about those dreams that you wouldn't dare tell anyone about because you don't even believe that they will come to pass yourself?

They were but mere fleeting thoughts that passed through your mind, and when you ponder on them, you feel exceedingly joyful and your stomach begins to turn because of the tiny possibility that your thoughts could become a reality. But then, the thought passes, and the reality of the day sets in; you begin to feel the pressure of bills, work, and family gnawing at the base of your neck. You resign that fleeting thought and return to the familiarity of your ordinary pre-planned life.

Yes, you know what I'm referring to because just as I've explained it, you remembered that moment in time where the thought of something amazing quickly left your mind.

I know that I've buried more than one dream in my lifetime. I have ordered the flowers and orchestrated the guest list for the service; I made sure to invite my will, emotions, and my faith to these funeral processions so that they, too, will know that some things are just not possible. My doubt had become greater than the reality of my true identity and because of that, I put my dreams to rest! "RIP Dreams!" was always what I wrote on the tablet of my mind. My only glimpse of hope was to one day wake up to the fact that just because I've buried my dreams doesn't mean that they will not happen. Just because I'd given up on waiting for some things to materialize didn't mean that they weren't going to come. For me to resurrect the faith of my dead dreams, I had to believe again. I had to know who I was for real this time. Not because people told me who I was, but because I know who I am.

I have a spectacular life to fulfill, one that encompasses peace and joy. I'm talking about real joy that tells a dream deferred, "You will be birthed, and I will do the mental work that is required to nurture you to maturity!"

Chapter Fourteen
The Love of Me

I had to learn how to love me and that started with recognizing the pain that I refused to allow myself to acknowledge. The same pain that I did not want to acknowledge was strangling the very life out of me. I decided to love myself past my pain. I decided to allow the Creator into my most painful memories, so that the path for my healing could be illuminated. I got up every morning with my pen ready to write. I began to write about and acknowledge the hurt in my life that I had been running from. I learned that the hurting little girl inside of me needed to be heard. And more than being heard, she needed to be held. I held her close and cared for her like I cared so much for others. I began to give her the love and attention she needed for her to grow and mature past the pain that kept her stuck. I began to love myself into maturity. I loved myself past my failures and mistakes. The love that I was searching for and wanting to give away to someone else, I began to give it to me. I started to forgive me, and I allowed myself the opportunity to make mistakes without criticizing myself to death. I now give myself grace. I have found that loving me can be allowed by me, unconditionally. If the Creator of the universe loves me regardless of my faults, then I need to stop tearing myself apart for shortcomings. I stopped criticizing myself and started to love who I was; I extend compassion to myself and started to love who I was on my way to becoming. My relationship with the Creator has shown me how to turn the very pain that used to hold me hostage into this amazing new life that I have now. Now, I accept the love of me! And now I am free to love others truly.

Learning to love ourselves enough to work through the hard and painful experiences in our lives is imperative to a healthy thought life. Actually, the very act of loving me required me to do the work.

I learned I had to love me first before I could love another. I decided my negative life experiences do not get to dictate my future any longer. It took some digging to uncover the real me, and I am still on this journey which, I believe, will be life-long. We can grow and evolve if we choose to or we can stay stuck where we are now and never search for any new knowledge of self. It has been a difficult road to unveiling me, but I am not turning back to the old me. I have learned to pray and ask God to help me on this journey of discovering the truth. He has truly been guiding me, and for that,

I will be forever grateful. I know now that reframing my thought life is repetitive work, so there are no shortcuts in this process. If you want a new thought life, it will require you to speak new thoughts daily. You can do this! Just like physical conditioning requires daily input so does the process of changing our thought life. It is equally important to envision yourself leaving the past in the past. The love of you is determined by your thought and actions towards yourself.

Describe the thoughts and actions that show how you love you.

_____

_____

_____

_____

_____

Are you a priority to you? Why? or Why not?

_____

_____

_____

_____

_____

Do you take a mental health day to ensure you are strong? If not, what would a mental health day look like for your

_____

_____

_____

_____

_____

Do you show care and concern for yourself the way you do for others? If not, why? If yes, how?

_____

_____

_____

_____

_____

Conclusion

Ernest Holmes writes in his book *The Science of the Mind*, "Life waits upon man to discover himself" … and I believe this is true. This means we can be whoever we desire to be, and we can have the things we desire to have- if we are ready to go and discover it.

We must consider "how" we think. What we believe is influenced by our current life situation, connections, and experiences. We are by-products of our beliefs and thoughts. In my case someone *taught* me how to be.

Ask yourself: What thoughts am I enforcing today that are the products of someone else's toxic thinking?

We must push the "Stop" button on our negative thinking patterns. Whether we admit it or not, our subconscious minds govern what we do and how we think. In life, things are constantly changing. I believe the Creator is giving us fresh intuitive ideas daily to change our lives. *Are we listening?* We can no longer defend or excuse negative thoughts and behaviors simply because it is what we are used to doing.

Are we missing the newness of today, stuck in the familiarity and comfort of yesterday's toxic habits and behaviors? New information is needed, which aims to assist us with creating new and healthy behaviors. Changing what we think is crucial to our development and freedom.

We cannot change the past, but we have the power to shape the future and to make it be whatever we want it to be. Questioning what we believe should be a normal occurrence and often it is the first step in creating a shift in personal beliefs. We have been given the power and the ability to think and create. This is an amazing gift to have if we learn how to use it for our benefit and the benefit of others. This gift must be protected, cherished and nurtured to maturity. The level of influence we have as human beings is powerful and deserves protection. Begin to challenge what you think. Pay attention to who you allow to come into your life and speak into your life.

I had to learn how to think and what to think. There is power in what we know, furthermore, there is an equal power in what we refuse to allow ourselves to accept or acknowledge. By not acknowledging damaging emotions, we choose to allow these emotions to wreak havoc in our minds, bodies and souls. We must take ownership of the truth of who we have become to know what we need to work on. Being truthful about how we feel can be difficult, but honesty is needed for us to become strong healthy thinking beings.

As written in *"Chronicles of Pain: Leaving the Pain of The Past Behind"*

"Your pain has purpose if you give it a voice!"

Made in the USA
Lexington, KY
04 November 2019